Railroad Fever

Songs, Jokes & Train Lore
by
Wayne Erbsen

R. Douglas Walker Collection

"The people up country are likewise agitated with the railroad fever." 1852

Order No. NGB-930   ISBN:1-883206-31-6

Contents

Photo by O. Winston Link

Are you Mad?

A passenger boarded the train at New York and firmly informed the porter that he needed to be awakened in time to get off at Buffalo. The porter solemnly swore it would be done.

When the man finally awoke and found out he'd missed his stop, he was mad as a boiled owl. To the furious passenger the porter replied, "You think you're mad? You should have seen the fellow I put off at Buffalo!"

Catching The Railroad Fever

"A Railroad Fever is pervading various portions of the state." 1880

The railroad fever that swept mid-nineteenth century America was not an isolated influenza, but a widespread epidemic. Few aspects of American life were left untouched. Within a few short years of America's introduction to railroads, life for most people would never be the same again. Now it was possible to travel at the unheard of speeds of twenty-five miles an hour. Goods which had traveled only by wagon could now be shipped by rail. Merchants who had once sold only to a local or regional market could now look to the four corners of the country for customers. The world suddenly got smaller.

Railroad Fever is not only about railroads as *machines*; it is also about *people*. It was *people* who built the railroads, laid the track, fired the engines and waited on the passengers. And because the railroad was on everyone's lips, it was people who created the lore, told the jokes, concocted the tall tales, believed in the superstitions and sang the songs of the railroad.

Each of the songs in **Railroad Fever** tells a different tale about what the railroad meant to Americans. In "Drill, Ye Tarriers," railroading was nothing but a dangerous job. If you survived being blown up by a stick of dynamite, you might lose your wages for the time you were in the air! Songs like "The Death of John Henry," and "Paddy Works on the Railroad" tell of the human toil required in building the railroad. To others, the railroad meant escape from lost love ("Early Morning Train," "Kansas City Railroad,") or a bad case of the blues ("The Railroad Blues," "Blue Train"). Many singers found that singing about railroads was almost as exhilarating as riding on one.

The spell that railroad fever cast over late 19th and early 20th century America is not even a memory for those of us now living in the age of astronauts and computers. Those early days are gone. But we can relive the glory days of railroading by digging into the songs, the stories, the jokes and even the superstitions of those days gone by. We can catch the railroad fever.

Railroad Superstition
It is unlucky to leave the shade up while traveling on an evening train lest the passenger become "moonstruck."

Blue Train

Much of the heart-felt emotion that is at the core of American folk and country music is a celebration of pain. Singers delight in songs of departed lovers, longing for home and even songs of death and dying. It is the sad songs that tug at your heart; it is the sad songs that are cherished and remembered long after the more cheery songs are forgotten.

In American literature it is often the railroad that is used to haul off this load of suffering and torment. For over a hundred and fifty years songwriters have seized the railroad as the perfect vehicle to express their darkest feelings. It is in this tradition that I composed "Blue Train" while visiting Yellowstone National Park in July, 1997.

Dog Delays Train

The September, 1945 issue of Railroad Magazine reported the story of a dog delaying a train. A terrier refused to get off the track between Wilmington and Woburn, Massachusetts. Despite efforts to shoo him away, the dog refused. By inching along and making twelve stops, the delayed train finally reached Woburn at which time the dog calmly trotted off.

Blue Train

Blue train, blue train,
Shovel in a little more coal.
Blue train, blue train,
I kinda got the itch to go.
I'll rattle down to Memphis
If I have to ride the blinds,
Blue train, blue train,
Take me down the railroad line,
Take me down the railroad line.

Blue train, blue train,
I'm leavin' this lonesome town.
Blue train, blue train,
I won't be hanging around.
When you take me southbound
All the troubles won't be mine,
Blue train, blue train,
Take me down the railroad line,
Take me down the railroad line.

Union Pacific laborers

Blue train, blue train,
All I've got is what I've lost.
Blue train, blue train,
I know when I've been bossed.
I don't care where you take me
The past is all behind,
Blue train, blue train,
Take me down the railroad line,
Take me down the railroad line.

The Race of the Century

"What happened to you?" a man asked his worn-out looking friend.
"I went down to watch the race of the century between a locomotive and a race horse. While I was bending down to tie my shoe, some nearsighted fool strapped a saddle on my back, put a bit in my mouth and got on. Then I heard a shot, a lot of commotion, and then some fool started kicking me in the side, so I ran."
"What happened then?" asked the breathless friend.
"I *won*."

What Time Does Your Turnip Say?
Some railroad men referred to their pocket watch as a "turnip."

The Death of John Henry

Melody Copyright © 1997 by Wayne Erbsen • Fracas Music Co. BMI

Perhaps America's most well-known ballad, "John Henry" freezes in song the events that took place at the Big Bend tunnel in Summers County, West Virginia around 1870-72. "The Death of John Henry," a variant of the more common ballad, was first recorded by Uncle Dave Macon in April, 1927 for Vocalion. To add to the continuing saga, here is my own version of "The Death of John Henry." It was created by gathering verses from a variety of sources which I sing to a new melody, set in a minor key.

Peo-ple out west heard of Jo-hn Hen-ry's death, Could-n't hard-ly st-ay in bed; Mon-day morn-ing on that east_ bound train, I'm go-in' where John Hen-ry fell dead, Goin' where John Hen-ry fell dead.

John Henry told his shaker,
"Shaker, you'd better pray
For if I miss this little piece of steel,
Tomorrow be your buryin' day
Tomorrow be your buryin' day."

Passenger: "Porter, who shined my shoes last night?"
Porter: "I most certainly did, sir. What seems to be the trouble?"
Passenger: "One of my shoes is brown and the other is black."
Porter: "That's funny. A man got off at Buffalo who complained of the very same thing.[6]"

"What can be more palpably absurd than the prospect held out of locomotives travelling twice as fast as stagecoaches?"
The Quarterly Review, England, March, 1825.

The Death of John Henry

"Travel makes a wise man better but a fool worse." Thomas Fuller (1732)

John Henry hammered on the right hand side,
The steam drill was on the left,
"Before I let that steam drill beat me down,
I'll hammer my fool self to death,
I'll hammer my fool self to death."

John Henry he told his captain,
"I am a Tennessee man,
Before I let that steam drill beat me down,
I'll die with a hammer in my hand,
Die with a hammer in my hand."

John Henry he hammered in the mountain,
'Til his hammer it caught on fire;
Very last words I heard him say,
"Cool drink of water 'fore I die,
Cool drink of water 'fore I die."

They carried John Henry to the graveyard,
They looked at him good and long;
Very last words that his wife said to him,
"My husband, he is dead and gone,
My husband, he is dead and gone."

Tom L. Sink Collection

Durham & Southern Railway

Railroad Superstition
It is unlucky to sleep in an upper berth.

The First Great Train Race

"If railroads are not built, how shall we get to heaven in season?"
Henry David Thoreau

It was August 28, 1830. Two parallel tracks were laid for the race of the century between the newly constructed steam locomotive *Tom Thumb*, and a horse named Gray. Each pulled a passenger car. With a snort of one and a puff of the other, the race was on.

"At first the horse had the best of it, and was perhaps a quarter mile ahead. Then the safety-valve on the engine lifted, and the thin blue vapor issuing from it showed an excess of steam. The blower whistled, the steam blew off in vapory clouds, the pace increased, the passengers shouted, the engine gained on the horse, soon it passed him. The lash was plied - the race was neck and neck, nose and nose. Then the engine passed the horse, and a great hurrah hailed the victory. But it was not repeated; for just at this time, when the Gray master was about giving up, the band which drove the pulley which moved the blower, slipped from the drum. The safety-valve ceased to scream, and the engine, for want of breath, began to wheeze and pant.

"In vain, Mr. Cooper, who was his own engineer and fireman, lacerated his hands in attempting to replace the band upon the wheel. In vain, he tried to urge the fire with light wood. The horse gained on the machine and passed it. Although the band was presently replaced, and steam again did its best, the horse was too far ahead to be overtaken, and came in the winner of the race. But the real victory was with Mr. Cooper, notwithstanding. He had held fast to the faith that was in him, and he demonstrated its truth beyond peradventure."[10]

MANCHESTER LOCOMOTIVE WORKS, MANUFACTURERS OF LOCOMOTIVES AND The Amoskeag Steam Fire Engines.

ARETAS BLOOD, SUPT. MANCHESTER, N.H. · **MANCHESTER, N.H.** · WM. G. MEANS, TREAS. 40 WATER ST. BOSTON.

Railroad Superstition
It is unlucky to sit backwards on a train.

Fishing With Dynamite

Besides being known as one of America's greatest fiddlers, Fiddlin' Arthur Smith loved to fish. One time while fishing on Trace Creek, about five miles out of Waverly, Tennessee, he got a little impatient, and decided to get his limit quick by using a stick of dynamite. To mask the sound of the explosion, he tried to time it so the charge would go off at the same time that a big freight train rumbled over the huge trestle. As luck would have it, the charge didn't go off as planned, and the train was long gone by the time the explosion went off. When the dynamite finally exploded, it announced to everybody in the county that Fiddlin' Arthur Smith had caught his limit at last.

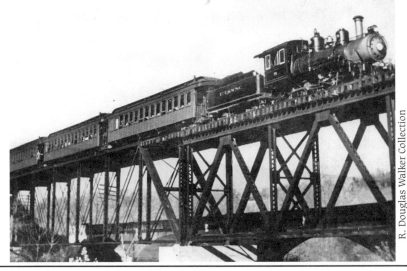

R. Douglas Walker Collection

Trouble?

A man and his teenage son were having an argument aboard a west bound train. A lady sitting right behind them objected to the noise. "If you don't stop yelling," she promised, "I will make trouble for you."

"Look, lady," said the man, "My wife just ran away with the iceman, the bank foreclosed yesterday on my mortgage, we are on the wrong train, and my son just dropped our tickets down the toilet. And *you're* going to make trouble for *me*?"[24]

Railroad Superstition

To ward off unwelcome advances from a suitor, tie one of his socks to a freight train.

Down at Dinah's Diner

If I could only ride the time train back to the glory days of railroading, my first stop would be a diner frequented by railroad men. As I slide onto an empty counter stool, I can smell the coffee, hear the bacon frying, and see a busy waitress skillfully carrying an armload of steaming platters to a table of hungry train men. Her customers are a true cross section of American railroaders. On a single morning she might serve an entire section crew of gandy dancers, track foremen, assorted brakemen, switchmen, firemen, engineers and conductors.

"Down at Dinah's Diner" is my attempt to capture in song the images of an old-time railroad diner. Written for this book and for the recording entitled **"Railroad Fever"** that accompanies it, the melody was borrowed from a 1904 ragtime composition by Thomas S. Allen entitled "By the Watermelon Vine, Lindy Lou."

Please pass the gravy.

RAILROAD DINER LINGO

A *mogul with two headlights*: Ham 'n eggs
Blanket the headlights: Eggs over easy
Running orders: Wheat cakes and coffee
A *hotbox, and have it smokin'*: A steak well-done
A *wreck on the mainline*: Scrambled eggs
Switch list: Menu
Cut the cow car off the java train: Black coffee
Life preservers: Donuts
Battleships: Pork chops
Murphies on the main line: Fried potatoes[20]

Railroad Superstition
If you mention your destination, you must knock on wood.

Down at Dinah's Diner

Copyright © 1997 by Wayne Erbsen • Fracas Music Co. BMI

Down at Di-nah's Di-ner where the freight trains are roll-in' I do the cook-in'. In the kitch-en, fry-in' chick-en, ev-ery morn-ing, clock a-tick-in', You'll find me there. I pour the cof-fee and I sling the hash, I wash the dish-es and take out the trash, I bake the bis-cuits and roll out the dough, So the rail-road boys will know,

Chorus

At Di-nah's, Di-nah's "What's it goin' to be bub?" Di-nah's, Di-nah's "Give me the ham." All the train crews say "Hey!"____ When it comes____ to pay day, "I wan-na eat at Di-nah's, it's the best food in the land."

Down by the switch yard,
It's not so very hard,
To smell the coffee.
Bacon cookin',
"Hey good lookin',
Whatcha got
     for breakfast cookin'?"
"What's it gonna be?"

The engineers, the brakemen,
Conductors and the firemen,
All eat at Dinah's.
The signal crew,
The porters too,
There's nowhere else,
What can they do?
But all stand in line.

11

The Wrong Man!

"Age is a bad traveling companion." Danish proverb

The train stopped at a small depot and down stepped a man carrying two heavy suitcases. He finally found his way to the only hotel in town but was disappointed to hear that all the rooms were full. Having no place to stay, he pleaded with the clerk, who found a good-natured retired Colonel who let him sleep in the extra bed in his room. Before he went to sleep, he asked the clerk to wake him up at 6:30 AM, as he had an early train to catch.

The next morning the bellhop greeted him with, "Good morning, Colonel." To his surprise, the doorman said the very same thing.

When he finally got on his train, he made his way to the washroom and looked in the mirror. *"My God,"* he said, *"They woke up the wrong man!"*

Menu on a Pullman Palace Car

Prairie Chicken	$1.00
Woodcock	$1.00
Pheasant, Snipe, Quail, Golden Plover, Blue Winged Teal, each	$1.00
Venison	60¢
Chicken, whole	75¢
Chicken, half	50¢
Sirloin Steak	50¢
Lobster and Broiled Ham or Bacon	40¢

"Railroad porters treat each individual piece of baggage as if they owed it a personal grudge." **Henry W. Lucy, 1885**

Strange But True Facts

- Pennsylvania has a town named "Railroad," but not an inch of track has ever run in or out of the town.

- A lonely telegrapher originally named the site of present day Harrisburg, Pennsylvania, "Enola." (Spell it backwards).

- The Lancaster & Reading Narrow Gauge railroad never ran anywhere near Reading and never had narrow-gauge track.

- After a disastrous train wreck on December 23, 1903, the dying conductor called to an injured baggageman to flag train #49, which would soon be bearing down on them. Not finding a lantern, he struck three matches, one at a time, and managed to warn the train, which stopped not three feet from the rear end of the wreck.

- One Pullman porter stripped a berth and found a diamond ring worth $120,000.

- Before the adoption of standard time in 1883, some stations had as many as six clocks mounted on their walls.

Whistle Talk

.	Apply brakes. Stop.
--	Release brakes.
-...	Flagman go back and protect rear of train.
----	Flagman return from west or south.
-----	Flagman return from east or north.
...-	Protect front of train.
--.-	Approaching highway crossing at grade.
-	Approaching stations, junctions and crossings.
..-	Approaching meeting, or waiting, points of trains.[16]

Railroad Superstition
It is unlucky to start a journey on Friday.

Buy a Mule!

"The railroad was nothing more than an incorporated octopus."

Canada Bill was an infamous card sharp who plied his trade aboard the Union Pacific railroad. Despite the efforts of railroad officials to oust him, Canada Bill seemed to outsmart railroad detectives at every turn. Though ruthless at three-card Monte, Canada Bill was never given to profanity and was generous to a fault.

One time, a young man lost all his money to Bill at cards. He left the smoking car but returned with his mother, who was in tears. Her son had gambled away their stake to begin homesteading. The mother begged for the return of their money, which was $110. Bill lectured the young man on the evils of gambling, then peeled from his roll three fifty dollar bills, which he handed to his mother. "But I have no change," the woman said. "Keep it all, and when you are settled on the homestead use the surplus to buy a mule."

Just An Average Tip

A man who never before had spent the night in a sleeping car took the train from New York to Boston. Just before the train reached South Station, the porter brushed his coat. "What's the average tip on this train?" asked the traveler.

"Two dollars," said the porter promptly.

"The traveler gave him two dollars and said, "You must make a lot of money being a porter."

'Not as much as you might think," answered the porter.

"You are the first *average* I've had in six months."[24]

Once I built a railroad, now it's done.
Brother, can you spare a dime?
*   - "Brother, Can You Spare a Dime?" by E.Y. Harburg*

Thomas Edison, News Butcher

"The incessant visitation of the train boy renders a quiet nap almost impossible." 1899

"While I was a newsboy on the Grand Trunk, I had a chance to learn that money can be made with a little careful thought. The Civil War was on and the Battle of Pittsburgh Landing, sometimes called the Battle of Shiloh, was in progress. I decided that if I could send ahead to outlying stations a hint of the big war news which I, there in Detroit, had learned was coming, I could do a better than normal business when I reached them."

Thomas A. Edison

"I therefore ran to the office of the *Detroit Free Press,* and asked Mr. Seitz, the man in charge, if he would trust me for a thousand newspapers. He regarded me as if perhaps I might be crazy, but referred me to Mr. Story. Mr. Story carefully considered me. I was poorly dressed. He hesitated, but finally told Mr. Seitz to let me have the papers."

"I got them to the station and into the baggage car as best I could and then attended to my scheme. All along the line I had made friends of the station-agents, who also were the telegraphers, by giving them candy and other things which a train-boy dealt in those days. I wired ahead to them, through the courtesy of the Detroit agent, who also was my friend, asking them to post notices that when the train arrived I would have newspapers with details of the great battle."

"When I got to the first station on the run, I found that the device had worked beyond my expectations. The platform literally was crowded with men and women anxious to buy newspapers. After one look at that crowd, I raised the price from five cents to ten and sold as many papers as the crowd could absorb. At Mount Clemons, the next station, I raised the price from ten cents to fifteen. The advertising worked as well at all the other stations. By the time I reached Port Huron, I had advanced the price of the *Detroit Free Press* for that day to thirty-five cents per copy and everybody took one."[2]

"Wake Up!"
To keep from falling asleep on duty, some engineers would balance a monkey wrench on their legs. If the wrench fell off, the noise would wake the sleeping engineer.

Drill, Ye Tarriers, Drill!

Credit for "Drill, Ye Tarriers, Drill" goes to Thomas F. Casey who apparently arranged and possibly composed new lyrics in 1888. Though he sang in theatrical productions in New York City, Casey earned his credentials for singing this song by working as a tarrier. Tarriers were the hard-working laborers who risked their lives drilling holes and planting dynamite to prepare the roadbed for the section gangs who laid the rails.

Ev - 'ry morn - in' at se - ven o' - clock, There's twen - ty tar - ri - ers on the rock, The boss comes a - long and he says, "Be still! And put all your pow - er in the cast - steel drill." Then *Chorus* drill, ye tar - ri - ers, drill, Drill, ye tar - ri - ers, drill, Oh it's work all day with - out sug - ar in your tay, Down be - hind the rail - way, And drill, ye tar - ri - ers, drill, and blast and fire._____

The boss was a fine man all around
But he married a great, big, fat fardown,
She baked good bread and baked it well,
And baked it hard as the hobs of H__l.

The new foreman is Dan McCann,
I'll tell you sure he's a blame mean man,
Last week a premature blast went off,
And a mile in the air went big Jim Goff.

When payday next it came around,
Poor Jim's pay a dollar short he found,
"What for?" says he, then came this reply,
"You were docked for the time you were up in the sky."

Signaling to the Train

The Fastest Train

"The railroad is life itself." J. Edward Hungerford

To pass the time, several passengers swapped tales of the fastest train they had known. One man claimed he once rode a train that went so fast that the telephone poles looked like a picket fence. Another went him one better and swore that on his fastest ride, the telephone poles looked just like a fine tooth comb. Finally, a little man in a bowler hat told his fastest train story: "We were rolling over the Kansas prairie so fast that alternating fields of corn and beans looked like one big mess of succotash!"[22]

Jerry Ledford Collection

Not Teetotalers

Trainmen, as a rule, were not teetotalers. Many saloons were named after its best customers: The Switch Key, The Time Card, The Crown Sheet, The Order Board, The Whistle Stop, The Semaphore, The Conductor's Rest, The Green Light, The Rear Shack, The Clear Track and The Roundhouse. In the 'eighties, beer could be bought for a nickel a glass.[7]

Railroad Superstition

To see corn in tassel as you ride home from a journey signifies an increase in your family.

Early Morning Train

"The railroad bids death and stagnation begone." J. Edward Hungerford

The pair of rails leading out of town has meant hope and promise for some, and a means of escape for others. "Early Morning Train" is my arrangement of Clarence Ashley's "Honey Babe Blues."

Well I'm lea-vin' on the ear-ly mo-r-ning train, I'm lea-vin on the ear-ly mo-r-ning train. And it's oh me, oh L-or-dy my, I'm leav-in on the ear-ly mo-r-ning train.

Oh, it's good gal, you ain't no friend of mine,
It's good gal, you ain't no friend of mine.

I'm goin' if I don't stay long,
I'm goin if I don't stay long.

Well, I ain't got no honey baby now,
No, I ain't got no honey baby now.

That old trouble has got a hold of me,
Oh trouble, won't you let my poor soul be.

Well, I'm leavin' on the early morning train,
I've got worries and troubles on my brain.

The Best & Cheapest Tippers

"Jimmy Durante was one of the best tippers there ever was. He always had a $10 bill in his hand no matter how many bags he had. The cheapest of them all was old man Rockefeller. You could carry five or six bags for him and he'd look you right in the eye and give you a dime." Oswald S. Thorne

His First Ride

"Traveling is a foretaste of hell." Turkestan proverb

An engineer discovered that one of the roundhouse mechanics had never been aboard a train. The engineer offered to take him out, and the mechanic reluctantly agreed. Just for sport, the engineer raced the train down the track at breakneck speeds to see how the mechanic would react. When they finally reached the roundhouse, the engineer asked the slightly green mechanic how he liked the ride. "I'd like to say 'Thanks' for both rides." "Both?" asked the puzzled engineer. "That's right," answered the slightly wobbly mechanic. *"My first and my last."*[24]

Rio Grande Southern

"The Wrong Side of the Tracks"

This phrase began in Abilene, Kansas when Wyatt Earp banned brothels and fandango houses to the south of Kansas Pacific Railroad's right of way.

Lost Teeth on the Train

"One time I was going West and I had a man named Green and his wife in my car. The first morning he comes to me and tells me he's in bad shape; he's lost his false teeth. He had his teeth in the sink, and when he let the water out, the teeth went out too. I told him he could go to the dining car and have some oatmeal, milk, toast...soft food. I told him he could make it for a couple of days. This was a man who liked his ham and steaks and such.

After he left the room, I took the screen out of the bottom of the sink, and found his teeth. I washed them off and carried them to the dining car. "Mr. Green, I thought you might want some ham or something, would you like to try my teeth and see if they fit?" He looked at them and said how they looked just about his size. I told him I got this extra set and you could use them for the rest of the trip; they're my good ones." He said, "I'll try them. I'm not eating oatmeal for this whole trip." He put them in and his wife, who was sitting there, almost fell out of her seat. I had told her, in the mean-time, what was going on, and I had to keep from laughing myself. He put them in and he had his breakfast and came back to the car. He said, "These teeth feel better than mine." I finally told them that they were his teeth, and I showed him the basin and how the screen was there to catch things. He thought that was the greatest thing in the world, how I'd kidded him." John E. Tibbs, porter.[9]

R. Douglas Walker Collection

"Traveling with children corresponds roughly to traveling third-class in Bulgaria." Robert Benchley

Strange Railroad Laws

- New Jersey law prohibits any railroad from running on Sunday.
- In Arizona, it is illegal to let water from a locomotive fall on the tracks.
- It is against the law in Maine to wear spike shoes in railroad stations or on rolling stock.
- It is illegal in Texas to gamble on a train. Texas law also requires one cuspidor for every three parlor-car seats.
- In Minnesota, a conductor may be jailed for failure to eject a gambler.
- Connecticut once passed a law making it illegal to ride on a train on Sunday.
- In Colorado, it is illegal to tip a Pullman porter.
- Michigan law makes it illegal to board a moving train.
- In Virginia, a steam train traveling after dark must be preceded by a man on foot or horseback carrying a lighted red lantern.
- In Indiana, locomotives must have glass windows. In Michigan, they must have curtains.
- It's against North Carolina law to drink milk on a train.
- Nebraska has a law that any animal hit by a train must be given first aid and then taken to the Humane Society.
- Florida law states that any passenger is required to assist the conductor in ejecting an unwanted passenger.
- Steam-driven vehicles were prohibited within the city limits of Albany and Buffalo.
- It is against the law to sneeze on a train in West Virginia.[16]

Bum Luck For Sam Bass

On the morning of April 10, 1878 the railroad messenger had a strange premonition that his train might be robbed, so he hid $30,000 in currency in the old potbellied stove in his car. His forebodings soon came true, for later that day Sam Bass and his gang of fifteen outlaws attempted to rob the train. The unsuspecting robbers made off with the total sum of $152.

Railroad Heroes

Johnny Bartholomew was the engineer at the throttle of the excursion train that left Virginia City, Nevada, on October 17, 1872. Close on his heels was No. 6, a regular train. Rounding a curve, Johnny looked ahead and saw flames leaping from the mouth of the American Flat tunnel. In an instant Johnny sensed the dire straits he was in. If he went headlong into the tunnel, he knew he and his fireman would surely meet a fiery death. If he jammed on the brakes, his train would be rear-ended by No. 6 and many passengers would die in the wreck. With little thought for his own life, Johnny chose the fiery tunnel. Luck was riding with him that day and Johnny and his train escaped without casualties, though the fire cost the railroad company half a million dollars.

Soon after this near catastrophe, G.H. Jennings composed a ballad about the heroism of Johnny Bartholomew, which included this verse:

> "Whistle down brakes," I first thought;
> Then, thinks I, "Oh boy, 'twon't do";
> And with hand on throttle an' lever
> I knew I must roll 'em through.
> Through the grim mouth of the tunnel,
> Through smoke an' flame as well,
> Right into the gateway of death, boys,
> Right smack through the jaws of hell![20]

Broke Again

A weary-looking businessman in a train station scribbled an urgent plea for help. "Dear Boss. I am flat broke, starving, and I've locked myself out of my hotel room. Send money right away."

As he handed it to the telegraph operator he said, "Please don't read it back to me; I don't believe I could handle it."

The Perfect Gentleman

The passenger car was very crowded. Sitting next to the window was a man with his head buried in his hands, crying his eyes out. The man sitting next to him tried to console him. "Are you sick, can I get anything for you?"

"No, it's nothing like that," the man answered. *"I just hate to see old ladies standing."*[24]

Strange But True Tales

In September, 1916, the Sparks World-Famous Circus rolled into the little town of Erwin, Tennessee. It arrived aboard one executive railroad car, two box cars and seven flat cars. The star of the show was Mary the elephant, who was billed as "The largest living land animal on earth."

Though normally well-mannered, Mary became violent and killed her trainer who had whipped her for not obeying him. When the massive elephant was finally contained, the circus management decided that Mary must be destroyed. The problem was, how to accomplish the grim task. No gun could be found that would be powerful enough to kill the huge beast. It was finally decided the only humane way to destroy Mary was to hang her from a 100-ton Clinchfield Railroad crane. On September 13, 1916, in front of a crowd estimated at 3,000 people, Mary was executed by hanging. It is the only known account of the lynching of an elephant.[17]

R. Douglas Walker Collection

Railroad Superstition
When traveling, put the germ of a bean in your shoe to keep from getting tired.

The Hell-Bound Train

Often sung at old-time camp meetings, the "Hell-Bound Train" has been attributed both to the cowboy preacher J.W. Pruitte and to F.M. Lehman. Its first known printing was in the *Ft. Gibson Post*, April 8, 1909, and was included in John Lomax's 1916 "bible" of cowboy music, *Cowboy Songs and Other Frontier Ballads*. All Aboard!

A Tex-an cow-boy on a bar-room floor Had drank so much he could hold no more.

He fell asleep with a troubled brain
To dream he rode on the Hell-bound train.
The engine with murderous blood was damp
And the headlight was a big brimstone lamp.

The imps for fuel were shoveling bones
And the furnace rang with a thousand groans.
The boiler was filled full of lager beer
And the Devil himself was the engineer.

The passengers they were a mixed-up crew,
Church member, atheist, Gentile, and Jew.
There were rich men in broadcloth and poor in rags
Handsome girls and wrinkled hags.

With red men, yellow men, black, and white,
All chained together, a fearful sight.
The train rushed on at an awful pace,
The sulphurous fumes scorched their hands and face.

A train is just a group of "big stages hung on to one machine."
Davy Crockett

The Hell-Bound Train

Faster and faster the engine flew,
And wilder and wilder the country grew.
Brighter and brighter the lightning flashed,
And louder and louder the thunder crashed.

Hotter and hotter the air became,
'Til the clothes were burned from each shrinking frame.
Then out of the distance there rose a yell:
"Ha ha," said the Devil, "the next stop is Hell."

Then oh, how the passengers shrieked with pain,
And begged the Devil to stop the train.
But he capered about and danced with glee
And he laughed and mocked at their misery.

"My friends, you have paid for your seats on this road,
The train goes through with a complete load.
You've bullied the weak, you've cheated the poor,
The starving brother turned from your door."

"You've laid up gold 'til your purses bust,
And given free play to your beastly lusts.
The laborer always expects his hire,
So I'll land you safe in a lake of fire."

"Your flesh will scorch in the flames that roar,
My imps torment you forevermore."
Then the cowboy awoke with an anguished cry,
His clothes were wet and his hair stood high.

He prayed as he'd never prayed before,
To be saved from Hell's front door.
His prayers and pleadings were not in vain,
For he never rode on the Hell-bound train.

25

Railroad Oddities

•In 1955, a conductor on a Pennsylvania train honored a ticket presented by a lady whose father had purchased it in 1872.

•The average speed of a first-class Union Pacific train in the early 1870's was twenty-two miles an hour.

•Before the use of the telegraph, station agents often climbed up to lofty perches to scan the horizon for approaching trains.

Missouri Pacific's #152

•During World War II, many "combat railroaders" were known to have cooked their eggs on a coal shovel heated by locomotive steam.

•The capital of North Dakota was changed in 1873 to Bismarck when The Northern Pacific thought that naming it after Otto von Bismarck would entice German settlement (and money) into the territory.

•To get around an 1890's law forbidding operation of Sunday trains unless they carried livestock, one resourceful railroad carried a single mule aboard a stock car.

•In 1944, Andy Williams was only 14 years old when he became the Milwaukee road agent at Interior, S.D.[18]

•During World War II, elephants were used for switching on the Bengal & Assam Railway in India.

Railroad Superstition
Getting the wrong ticket at a railway station foretells that your train will meet with an accident.

Railroad Oddities

- Boys living along railroad tracks used to put an ear on a rail to tell if a train was coming and to estimate how long it would take to arrive.

- One forgetful passenger left behind a handbag containing jewels worth $125,000. An honest porter found the handbag containing the jewels and returned it to its owner. History didn't record if the porter received a tip.

- Railroad men were pondering how to get a circus giraffe under a low bridge. They finally managed to get the giraffe past the bridge by dropping some carrots on to the floor of the car. When the hungry animal lowered his head to gobble the carrots, the engineer received a signal to advance the car past the bridge.

- In Colorado, a herd of cattle attacked a train and overturned the caboose.

No Whiskers!

In the mid to late 19th century, a man wasn't fully dressed unless he wore a hat and a beard. During the panic of 1873, many railroad workers were laid off and a new "brass hat" was brought in to the Reading, Pennsylvania railroad. Among his first "official" acts was to order the remaining workers to shave their beards. Though

unorganized, all the workers immediately walked off the job. When they left, they took with them the coupling links and pins and the engine side rods. With the railroad at a standstill, management was frantic to negotiate, but since the workers weren't organized, they could find no one to negotiate with. They finally managed to get the workers back on the job by promising to end the ban on whiskers.

He's Coming to Us Dead

A composer like Gussie L. Davis could really hurt a feller with songs which tugged at the tenderest heart strings. As the composer of "He's Coming to Us Dead," Davis knew first-hand the pleasures and sorrows of life on the railroad from his years as a Pullman porter. To complete his credentials as one of the most gifted song writers of the 1890's, Davis also worked as a janitor at the Cincinnati Conservatory of Music. Besides being schooled in the use of a broom and dust mop, Davis used his time wisely to sweep up bits of music training which would serve him well in composing popular songs of the day. His other well-known compositions included "In the Baggage Coach Ahead" (see p. 35) and "The Red and Green Signal Lights" (see p. 58). "He's Coming to Us Dead" was first published in 1899 by F. A. Mills, the author of the popular cake-walk song, "At the Georgia Camp Meeting." It tells the gut-wrenching story of a father coming to pick up his deceased son at the express office, not the passenger depot.

One morn-ing when the of-fice had o-pened, A man quite old in years, Stood by the ex-press of-fice, Show-ing signs of grief___ and tears.

When the clerk approached him,
In trembling words did say,
"I'm waiting for my boy sir,
He's coming home today."

"Well, you have made a slight mistake,
And you must surely know,
This is a telegraph office, sir,
And not a town depot."

"If your boy is coming home"
The clerk in smiles did say,
"You'll find him with the passengers,
At the station just o'er the way."

He's Coming to Us Dead

"You do not understand me, sir,"
The old man shook his head,
"He's not coming as a passenger,
But by express instead."

"He's coming home to mother,"
The old man gently said.
"He's coming home in a casket, sir,
He's coming to us dead."

Then a whistle pierced their ears;
"The express train," someone cried;
The old man rose in a breathless haste
And quickly rushed outside.

Then a long white casket
Was lowered to the ground,
Showing signs of grief and tears
To those who'd gathered 'round.

"Do not use him roughly, boys,
It contains our darling Jack,
He went away as you boys are,
This way he's coming back."

"He broke his poor old mother's heart
Her fears have all come true,
She said this is the way that he'd come back
When he joined the boys in blue."

Johnny Appleseed's Alarm Clock

One of the trees said to have been planted by Johnny
Appleseed in the early 1800's grew so big that its branches nearly
touched passing trains of the Philadelphia & Reading Railroad. One
engineer devised a clever way to wake himself from his daily nap
while running his train between Mount Carbon and Port Richmond,
Pennsylvania. He stuck his feet out the window of his cab far
enough so that the branches of the famous apple tree would brush
his feet and wake him from blissful slumber.

Tall Tales of the Rails

Two Shots?

A robber was standing in irons in front of the judge. "You are accused of stealing a purse from a traveler at the train depot. How do you plead?"

"Innocent, judge," answered the prisoner. "I was merely taking a stroll when I heard two shots."

"Two shots?" asked the judge. "The policeman who apprehended you said he only fired one shot."

"No," answered the prisoner. "I distinctly remember hearing two shots. The first one was when the bullet passed me and the second was *when I passed it.*"

If The Shoe Fits

A retired shoe salesman was taking a trip by train. At nightfall, he climbed in his berth and began snoring loudly. Unable to stand the noise, another passenger picked up a shoe and threw it at him. The snoring man awoke with a jolt. He picked up the shoe, looked it over carefully and said, "I'm sorry; we are all out of your size."

Hard To Die

"One passenger wanted to commit suicide, so he ran a mile ahead and laid down on the track, but the train was so slow, he couldn't wait, as he had to get up to find something to eat."[4]

Nuthin' To It

A Southern Pacific express train sped along the edge of one of the biggest cattle ranches in Texas. A passenger gazed intently at the huge herds grazing near the right of way. When the train passed the end of the ranch, he turned to the man who occupied the seat with him and said, "Quite a herd of cattle on that ranch. I counted 11,442 head."

The man next to him looked at him in astonishment. "I am the owner of that ranch, and I know for certain that there are exactly 11,442 head of cattle out on that pasture. How in the world did you manage to count them from a train that is going sixty miles an hour?"

"Oh, it's easy enough, if you know the system," said the man. You just count their legs and divide by four."[24]

Railroad Superstition
Accidents occur in a series of three.

Tall Tales of the Rails

A guard from a lunatic asylum rushed up to the foreman of a railroad crew repairing a section of track.

"I am looking for an escaped lunatic. Did he pass this way?"

"What did he look like?" asked the foreman.

"He's very short, rather thin, and weighs about 350 pounds."

The foreman looked puzzled. "How can a man be short and thin and still weigh 350 pounds?"

"Don't ask me," said the guard, *"I told you he was crazy."*[24]

THE FORTUNE TELLER

A passenger named Wilson noticed a fortune telling machine in the depot while he waited for an express train. "Why not?" he said, inserting a penny in the slot. The fortune teller's eyes lit up, its mouth opened, and out dropped a fortune. Mr. Wilson retrieved a card that read, "Your name is Wilson and you weigh 156 lbs."

"It can't be," marveled Mr. Wilson. "No one knows I'm even here."

He tried again, and the same thing happened, "Your name is Wilson and you weigh 156 lbs."

Mr. Wilson was flabbergasted. He turned around and saw a young Irishman standing nearby.

"Please," he asked the man. "Let me buy you a free fortune." The Irishman agreed, and Mr. Wilson put another penny in the slot. His card read, "Your name is O'Flanery and you weigh 175 lbs."

Mr. Wilson could not believe his eyes. Just to make sure the fortune teller could repeat the magic once again, he put yet another penny in the slot. This time the card bore a longer message, "You crazy nut. *You have just missed your train."*[24]

Tall Tales of the Rails

Wrong Street

The conductor came to a lady that had a big boy, dressed in knee pants. He looked like he ought to have been moving pianos or tending bar. The conductor said, "Lady, how old is the boy?" She said, "He is just in the neighborhood of eight." The conductor said, He may be in that neighborhood, *but he ain't even on that street."*[11]

Crazy As A Loon

"This is a sad case," said the attendant at an insane asylum, pausing before a padded cell. "There is no hope for the patient."

"What seems to be the trouble with him?" asked a visitor.

The attendant shook his head and said, "He thinks he can understand an Erie time-table."

Photo by O. Winston Link

And That's The Truth!

"Our train went so slow it just barely nudged an old cow walking leisurely down the track. Before long, her tail got caught in the cowcatcher. When the engineer blew the whistle, she spooked and ran off down the track dragging the train behind her."[4]

Tall Tales of the Rails

The World's Slowest Train

"One time I rode on the world's slowest train. It stopped at every house. When it come to a double house, it stopped twice. They made so many stops I said, "Conductor, what have we stopped for now?" He said, "There are some cattle on the track." We ran a little ways further and stopped again. I said, "What is the matter now?" He said, "We have caught up with those cattle again."[4]

The Goat That Flagged The Train

There was a man named Joseph Dunn
Who bought a billygoat just for fun.
One day the goat, prone to dine,
Ate a red shirt right off the line.

Then Dunn to the goat did say:
"Your time has come; you'll die today."
And took him to the railroad track,
And bound him here upon his back.

As the train approached with rush and roar,
Goat used his brain as ne'er before,
And with a mighty shriek of pain,
Coughed up the shirt and flagged the train.[16]

Slang for Locomotive

Battleship, battle wagon, bobtail, bull, camel, coffeepot, dead engine, eight-wheeler, fantail, galloper, girl, goat, goo-goo eyes, grasshopper, groundhog, hog, iron hog, iron horse, junk pile, kettle, loco, lokey, Mother Hubbard, mudhen, muzzle-loader, oiler, old girl, paddle wheel, peanut roaster, pig, pig iron, pony, rat crusher, rust pile, sacred cow, scrap pile, sidewinder, smoker, snuff dipper, stack of rust, steam horse, steam wagon, tea kettle, tramp.[14]

Yesterday's Train

Arkansas acquired the reputation of having trains so slow that a snail could overtake them. One day a frequent traveler on an Arkansas railroad hailed the conductor as the train was approaching the station.

"I say, there, conductor. Please accept this fine cigar as a token of my admiration."

"What's this for?" asked the surprised conductor.

"For getting this train in right on time" answered the beaming traveler.

"Thanks so much," said the conductor, extending a hand to accept the cigar."

"There's only one problem," confessed the nervous conductor.

"What's that?" asked the traveler suspiciously.

"This is yesterday's train."

Smithsonian Photo #20380

The Whisk-Broom Blues

Listerine was advertised in *Railroad Magazine* in the early 1940's with a picture of a Pullman porter playing a whisk broom as if it were a banjo. These are the words he sang:

> When dandruff flakes on the coats fell down,
> What tips! Oh Man! and was I flush?
> But now that Listerine's a roun'
> There's dog-gone little left to brush!
> So I got them whisk-broom blues
> Them thin dime blues!

Railroad Superstition

To ward off bad luck when traveling, turn some of your clothing inside out.

In the Baggage Coach Ahead

In the 1890's, the narrow, back-streets of New York City were home to a flourishing song publishing industry known as Tin-Pan Alley. Hopeful songwriters trooped from one publisher to another with dreams of having their newest tear-filled ballads accepted for publication.

Among those facing rejection at every door was a black composer by the name of Gussie L. Davis. Some years before, he had worked as a Pullman porter and heard a true story from another porter that made his heart sink. A father aboard a passenger car was trying in vain to quiet his crying infant. When passengers objected to the noise, they learned that the baby's deceased mother was in the baggage coach ahead. Davis later turned his story into a ballad and tried desperately to get it published. After meeting rejection after rejection, Davis finally arrived at the publishing house of Howley, Haviland & Co. Meeting again with rejection, Davis offered to sell the song for a mere pittance, and they reluctantly agreed to purchase all the rights. To their surprise, "In the Baggage Coach Ahead" soon became a hit by Imogene Comer, the "Queen Regent of Song," on her tour with Harry Williams' "Own Company." Gussie L. Davis, though deprived of any royalty for his song, did get composer credit, and he eventually became one of the most well-known songwriters of the 1890's. This version of the song is from Ernest Thompson's September 24, 1924, recording for Columbia.

The End of the Line

After a huge wreck, a passenger car careened down the side of a mountain. Among the passengers who rolled out was a very small man and a very large woman. As they tumbled down the embankment, they kept bumping into one another. When they finally stopped rolling, the little man was on the bottom and the big woman was on top of him. As rescue workers approached the pair, the muffled voice of the man was heard to say, "I'm afraid, madam, you'll have to get off here, as this is as far as I go!"[22]

Photo by Wayne Erbsen

In the Baggage Coach Ahead

On a dark storm-y night as the train rat-tled on, All the pass-en-gers all gone to bed, Ex-cept a young man with a babe in his arms Who sat with a bowed-down head. The in-no-cent one began cry-ing just then, As though its poor heart would break; An ang-ry man said, "Make that child stop its noise, For it's keep-ing us all a-wake." As the train rolled on and on a hus-band sat in tears, Think-ing of the hap-pi-ness of just a few short years; For the ba-by's face brings pic-tures of the che-rished hope that's dead, But ba-by's cries can't wa-ken her in the bag-gage coach a-head.

In the Baggage Coach Ahead

"Take it out," said another, "don't keep it here,
We've paid for our berths and want rest;"
But never a word said the man with the child,
As he fondled it close to his breast.
"Oh where is it's mother? Go take it to her,"
A lady then softly said.
"I wish I could," was the man's sad reply,
"She's dead in the coach ahead."

Every eye filled with tears as his story he told,
Of a wife who's so faithful and true;
He told how he had saved up his earnings for years,
Just to build up a home for two.
How heaven had sent them a sweet little babe,
Their young happy lives to bless;
His heart seemed to break when he mentioned her name,
And in tears tried to tell the rest.

Every woman arose to assist with the child,
There were mothers and wives on that train;
And soon the little one was sleeping in peace,
Without any thought, sorrow, or pain;
Next morning at the station he bade them goodbye,
"God bless you," he softly said.
Each one had a story to tell in their homes,
Of the baggage coach ahead.

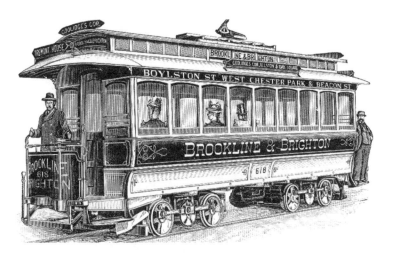

Jordan is a Hard Road to Travel

D aniel D. Emmett, remembered as the author of "Dixie," "The Blue-Tailed Fly" and "Old Dan Tucker," composed "Jordan is a Hard Road to Travel" in Cincinnati, Ohio in 1853. It was soon picked up by other black-faced minstrels and sung everywhere from the concert halls of the east coast to the gold fields of California. Many parodies of the song were written, including the popular Civil War song "Richmond is a Hard Road to Travel." In the late 1850's Jacob P. Weaver borrowed Emmett's tune and added his own set of words which he called "Rail-Road Song." It paints a vivid picture of the railroad life through the eyes of the railroad workers themselves. I have added Emmett's chorus back on the song. Thanks to Norm Cohen for reprinting it in his book, *Long Steel Rails*.

"Is That You, Joe?

Two men accidentally bumped into each other in a crowded train station. Excusing themselves, the first man said, "Why it's Joe Sellers! I haven't seen you in years. You're looking good! I see you've lost twenty pounds, dyed your hair, grown a beard and you must have grown two inches."

The second man stepped back, and replied, "I'm *not* Joe Sellers." The first man then said, "You've even changed your name!"

Railroad Superstition
It is unlucky to disturb a robin's nest.

Jordan is a Hard Road to Travel

There's the engineer too, he's the best of the crew,
He tried his water accordin',
If his pumps work true, he's nothing more to do,
For to land him on the other side of Jordan.

Common brakemen think they've a mighty good job,
But that all depends upon the boarding,
Nine dollars a week and not a bit of sleep,
For to land them on the other side of Jordan.

There's the hind brakesman too, he's nothing for to brag,
If he can't make his premium accordin',
They'll give him his time and put him off the line,
And they'll send him on the other side of Jordan.

There's the conductor too, he's the worst of the crew,
He's charged with the whole train accordin',
If a car breaks down he's got to run around,
For to land them on the other side of Jordan.

R. Douglas Walker Collection

Railroad Superstition
It is good luck to have your traveling gown trimmed with leather.

The ABC's of XYZ

A passenger was bragging that he knew the abbreviation for every train in America. A retired railroad man sitting nearby looked over at him and called out "IC." The passenger shot right back with "Illinois Central."

"D & R. G."

"Denver & Rio Grande," came the answer.

"A.T. & S.F."

"Atchison, Topeka and Santa Fe," answered the traveler with a smirk.

In desperation, the railroad man tried once more.

"C.B. & Q."

The passenger paused, looked sick, and in a weak voice answered with *"Chicago, Baltimore and Cuba."*

Harold K. Vollrath Collection

The Power of a Free Pass

Though Frank and Jesse James robbed at least seven trains between 1866 and 1882, they never held up the Chicago, Burlington & Quincy Railroad, which ran right through their hometown of Kearney, Missouri. And why not? As a preventive measure, railroad officials gave their mother a free pass to ride their trains.

Railroad Firsts

1804 1st American steam locomotive, built by Oliver Evans.
1826 1st horse-pulled railway car, *The Granite Railway.*
1830 1st steam locomotive put in regular service,
    The Best Friend of Charleston.
1830 1st common-carrier, *Baltimore & Ohio.*
1831 1st mail carried on railroad, South Carolina.
1832 1st railroad accident, on *The Granite Railway.*
1837 1st locomotive whistle.
1858 1st Pullman sleeper goes into operation.
1869 1st transcontinental railroad completed.
1856 1st railroad bridge built across the Mississippi River.
1866 1st train robbery, by Gus Tristam.

The Great Railroad Snorer

A well-dressed gentleman boarded the evening train, tucked himself into his berth, and immediately began snoring. The volume of his snoring was enough to wake the dead. Even people in adjoining cars were awakened by his incessantly loud and constant snoring. Finally, the man turned over, snorted a few times, and then there was a brief moment of blissful silence. A preacher in a nearby berth who had been kept awake by the snoring, called out to the amusement of the other hopeful sleepers, *"Thank God, he's dead!"*

Not For Sissies

Railroad work was second only to steel mills in the number of fatalities of its workers. In 1900 alone, there were 2675 railroaders killed and another 41,142 injured. This was about equal to British army losses in the three-year Boer War.

"Cleanliness is Next to Godliness"

Operating on the principle that "Cleanliness is next to Godliness," many communities in the early days of railroading forbad trains from running through town for fear that the soot from passing locomotives would foul windows. Special teams of horses stood ready to tow trains past the city limits.

Kansas City Railroad

"Such things as railroads are impossibilities." Ohio School Board, 1828

Close kin to "Goin' Down the Road Feelin' Bad," this version of "Kansas City Railroad" was recorded by Riley Puckett on March 30, 1934. Though the tune has stayed pretty much the same over its long life, it has had more sets of words than Carter's got liver pills! Not only has it been sung as a railroad song, but older versions relate to the early days of steamboating.

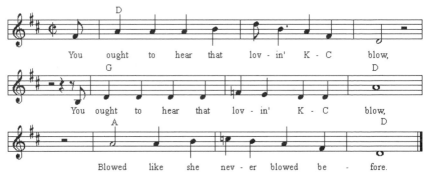

You ought to hear that lov - in' K - C blow,
You ought to hear that lov - in' K - C blow,
Blowed like she nev - er blowed be - fore.

Goin' down that road feelin' bad,
Oh I'm goin down that road feelin' bad,
Lord I ain't gonna be treated this a-way.

Ain't got no lovin' baby now,
Lord I ain't got no lovin' baby now,
Lord I ain't gonna be treated this a-way.

My baby left me on that old KC,
My baby left me on that old KC,
I'll be riding if she don't come back to me.

Fred Harvey

MEAL PRICES

LUNCHEON
45¢

BREAKFAST
25¢, 35¢ & 45¢

DINNER
40¢, 45¢ & 55¢

Hand me down my long distance phone,
Hand me down my long distance phone,
Ain't got no lovin' baby now.

I'm goin' where the chilly winds don't blow,
Goin' where the chilly winds don't blow,
Lord I ain't gonna be treated this a-way.

Goin' down the road feelin' bad,
Goin' down the road feelin' bad,
Cause I ain't gonna be treated this a-way.

Run-Away Locomotive

On a Sunday evening in 1952, a railroad worker was on his way home near Bennetsville, South Carolina when he spotted the ghostly sight of a train running without lights. Looking closer, he recognized the locomotive as the *One Spot*, and was shocked to see that the train was running without a crew. He quickly telephoned the road's master mechanic, who chased the run-away train for eight miles and finally managed to bring it to a stop. The cause of the unplanned solo journey was attributed to steam leaking into the cylinders.

R. Douglas Walker Collection

Home Sweet Home!

In the days before diesel, many engineers fashioned their own train whistles. You could often tell who was at the throttle by the unique sound of the whistle. Some engineers were experts at playing tunes with their whistles. "Whistling Bill" Wardoff, a Reading, Pennsylvania engineer, was adept at playing "Home Sweet Home." During World War I, his run took him near an army base close to the New Jersey seacoast. His version of "Home Sweet Home" made so many soldiers homesick that the commanding officer asked the railroad management to instruct "Whistling Bill" to refrain from whistling this tune within earshot of the base.

> **Passenger: "I want to catch a late train to New York."**
> **Station Agent: "Take No. 9. It's as late as any."**

The Little Red Caboose

Far from being just a place to hang your hat, the caboose was also a shelter from a storm, a place to light your lantern or tally your way-bills. At times it served as mess-hall, dormitory, lookout, storeroom, and office for the conductor.

"The Little Red Caboose" is a take-off on a song by William S. Hays entitled "The Little Log Cabin in the Lane" (1871). His other well-known compositions included, "The Drummer Boy of Shiloh" (1862), "We Parted by the Riverside" (1866), "I'll Remember You, Love, in My Prayers" (1869), and "Molly Darling" (1871).

We are jol-ly A-mer-i-can rail-road boys and brak-ing is our trade, we're al-ways on the go both day and night; Throw-ing switch-es, mak-in' flag-stops, a-long the line we go, and to see that all the train is made up right. You bet we're al-ways rea-dy when called up-on to go, no mat-ter whet-her sun-shine or in rain, and a jol-ly crew you'd find us if you will come and see, in the lit-tle red ca-boose be-hind the train.

The Caboose

If the number of nicknames is a measure of affection, then the caboose has earned a warm place in the heart of many a railroadman: animal car, ape wagon, bazoo wagon, cage, chariot, chuck wagon, clown wagon, cook shack, coop, cracker box, crib, crow's nest, crumb box, crummy, doghouse, doodlebug, flophouse, flop wagon, glory wagon, go-cart, hack, hearse, hut, louse cage, monkey cage, palace, parlor, perambulator, possum belly, shanty, sun parlor, zoo.

The Little Red Caboose

Two red lights we hang on each side, another one behind,
In the evening when the sun is almost gone;
You bet the lad that rides ahead will keep it in his mind
To see that all the train is coming on.
When we are near the station, how thoughtless out we go,
All a-singin' or whistlin' some refrain;
Then we climb out on the hurricane deck and leave our coats inside
Of the little red caboose behind the train.

This little car we speak of, more precious and more dear,
Than all the other coaches on the line;
And the reason why we tell you, because it is our home
We always try to keep it looking fine.
Although we have no fashion lights, no velvet cushion chairs,
Everything inside just neat and plain;
There's many an honest heart that beats beneath that rusty roof,
In the little red caboose behind the train.

> So here's success to all the boys that ride upon the cars,
> May happiness always with you remain,
> And a jolly crew you'd find us if you will come and see
> In the little red caboose behind the train.

R. Douglas Walker Collection

Porter: *Do you want to sleep with your feet to the engine?"*
Passenger: *"No, they're not long enough."*[6]

The Red Light

Not long after the Civil War, Kansas cowtowns like Abilene, Dodge City, Hays and Wichita were bustling centers of activity as trains carried Texas Longhorn cattle to hungry markets in the east. With a rough and ready population composed mainly of single men, saloons and bordellos sprang up everywhere. When railroad men visited the ladies of the night, they often hung a red lantern outside, in the event they were needed to make up a train. The area of town lighted by these lanterns soon became known as "Red Light Districts."

R. Douglas Walker Collection

Don't Jump!

Patrick O'Toole was hired as a brakeman in a mountainous section of Pennsylvania and was paid on the number of miles run. On one of his first trips, the engineer lost control of his train, and it went speeding down a dangerous grade at high speeds.

The conductor, sensing danger, saw O'Toole on the running board clinging for his life. Knowing O'Toole was new on the job, the conductor yelled, "Don't Jump! You'll be killed!"

O'Toole yelled back, "Do you think I'm fool enough to jump when I'm making money as fast as I am now?"[16]

Railroad Superstition
It is bad luck to let a woman enter a train first.

Train Trivia

- The longest stretch of straight track in the U.S. ran 78.86 miles from Wilmington to Hamlet, North Carolina.
- The state with the most miles of track is Texas -- 13,304 miles.
- The world's lowest point serviced by a railroad is near Zemach, Israel at 808.42 feet below sea-level.
- The shortest tunnel in America is the Bee Rock tunnel near Appalachia, Virginia. It measures 10 yards long.
- The longest railroad tunnel in America is the Cascade Tunnel on the *Great Northern* from Spokane to Seattle (2 miles, 1109 yards).
- The world's fastest train to date is France's *Train a Grande Vitesse* with speeds of 319 mph.

Railroad Nicknames

Leavenworth, Kansas & Western	L. K. & W.	Leave Kansas & Walk
Missouri & Northern Arkansas	M. & N. A.	May Never Arrive
Minneapolis & St. Louis	M. & St. L.	Misery & Short Line
Fort Smith & Western	F. S. & W.	Footsore & Weary
Newburgh, Dutchess & Ct.	N. D. & C.	Never Did & Couldn't
Georgia & Florida	G. & F.	Got Forgot
Carolina & Northwestern	C. & N. W.	Can't & Never Will
Maryland & Pennsylvania	M. & PA.	Ma & Pa
Hoosac Tunnel & Wilmington	H. T. & W.	Hoot, Toot & Whistle
		Hot Tea & Whiskey
		Hog-Tied & Weary
Houston, East & West Texas	H. E. & W.	Hell Either Way You Take It
Nevada, California & Oregon	N. C. & O.	Narrow, Crooked & Ornery
Delaware, Lackawanna & West	D. L. & W.	Delay, Linger & Wait
Missouri, Oklahoma & Gulf	M. O. & G.	Mostly on the Ground
Silver Spring, Ocala & Gulf	S.S.O. & G.	Sick, Sold Out & Gone

The Longest Train

This version of "The Longest Train," combines the words associated with "In the Pines" with the driving melody of "Fall on My Knees," from the music of Tommy Jarrell of Toast, North Carolina. The lyrics are as interchangeable as a nameless boxcar. They can be switched, almost in any order, to another train and just keep right on rolling.

Look up and down that long lo-ne-some road, Hang down your he-ad and cry, lit-tle girl, Hang down your he-ad and cry.

The longest train I ever saw,
Was nineteen coaches long, little girl,
Was nineteen coaches long.

The engine passed at six o'clock,
The cab passed by at nine,
The cab passed by at nine.

I wish to the Lord the train would wreck,
And break the fireman's neck, little girl,
And break the fireman's neck.

It's a long steel rail and a short cross tie,
I'm on my way back home, little girl,
I'm on my way back home.

If I'd a listened what mama said,
I'd never a-been here today, little girl,
I'd never a-been here today.

A lyin' around this old jail cell,
A-sleepin' my life away,
A-sleepin' my life away.

Porter: "Which way do you want to sleep, head first or feet first?"
Passenger: "I'd like to sleep all over at the same time."[22]

48

The World's Cheapest Tipper?

"Traveling people. They knew how to tip." Oswald S. Thorne, Porter

"Prophet Jones, the preacher from Detroit, was one you wanted to stay away from. He'd step off that train in his minks and diamonds. Medallions of gold hung around his neck with diamonds all around them. He would reserve the whole train for his disciples and what not. Maybe ten cars. They might have 400-500 bags. We had to carry those bags up to Vanderbilt Avenue where he would have ten, maybe more, limousines and buses for his people. When it came time to paying off the redcaps he was very cheap. Give you only what the going rate was for each bag, fifteen cents in those days."[9] Oswald S. Thorne, Pullman porter.

Collection of R. Douglas Walker

The Intelligence Test

A dim-witted engineer was worried sick when he heard that all engineers would have to take an intelligence test. Fearing the worst, he convinced the examiner to let him take the test on Sunday.

"OK," began the examiner, "This test has just one question. Imagine you are running a train from Rouses Point to Albany, stopping at Saratoga. Where would you stop, and where would you side track?"

The nervous engineer straightened up, cleared his throat, and finally answered, "I'd stop at Saratoga and Albany."

The examiner shot out of his seat and shouted, "You idiot, that's wrong! You'd have seven accidents. You've failed the test!"

"But sir," protested the engineer. "Didn't you say I'm running the train today?"

"That's right," answered the examiner.

"Today is Sunday. *Those other trains aren't running today.*"[21]

Railroad Superstition
To miss your train signifies a hasty quarrel about nothing.

Oh Yeah?

The governor of Texas was bragging to the governor of Arkansas that "My state is so big you can get on a train and travel two days and nights but when you wake up, you're still in Texas." The Arkansas governor rolled his eyes and said, *"Oh yeah? Well we've got trains like that in Arkansas, too."*

Big Ouch!

A story is told of one curious boy who barely escaped from the path of an oncoming train when he tried licking the frost off a rail and his tongue became stuck to it.[2]

Tasty Reward

A reward for the capture of suspected Southern Pacific train robbers Christopher Evans and Jon Sontag consisted of "Ten Dollars and an Oyster Supper."[2]

Blue Ridge Parkway

Green Bananas

A little old Scottish couple shared a seat on the train from Edinburgh to London. At every way-station the man would hop out of the train and buy two tickets for the next station. The conductor finally got tired of punching the tickets.

"Where are you two bound?" asked the conductor.

"London," answered the Scotsman.

"Then why don't you just buy two through tickets and save me all this bother?" asked the conductor.

"Ah" said the Scotsman. "At our age, we don't even buy green bananas."[24]

Railroad Superstition
It is bad luck to take an engine on its first trip on Fridays.

The Wrong Train

The Los Angeles Limited wasn't ten minutes out of the Chicago Union Station when a little old lady noticed a stranger in the front of the car whose head was buried in his hands. His shoulders shook as he cried his eyes out. Her motherly instincts kicked in but she resisted the impulse to comfort him. All that day and on into the next day, she watched him sniffle into his handkerchief. On the third morning, with the train almost to its destination, she couldn't stand it any longer. "My poor boy," she said as she patted him on the shoulder, "maybe if you talk about your troubles, you'll feel better."

With tears in his eyes the man looked up at her and said, *"For three days now I've been on the wrong train."*[24]

"My Dad is a Train"

The superintendent of an Oklahoma railroad was complaining to a friend about a farmer who claimed that the cow killed by his train was the finest in the land. His friend looked up at him and said, "There's nothing that improves the breed of livestock like crossing it with a locomotive."

> **You know you're old when a pregnant woman on a train gets up to give you her seat.**

Paddy Works on the Railway

T he Irish Potato famine of the 1830's and '40's brought to America's shores thousands of Irish immigrants who quickly attempted to join the work force. When they met with notices that read, "No Irish Need Apply," many signed on as laborers for the railroad, which always needed large numbers of workers. Though commonly sung as a sea shanty, "Paddy Works on the Railway" is a classic railroad song that goes back at least to the 1850's.

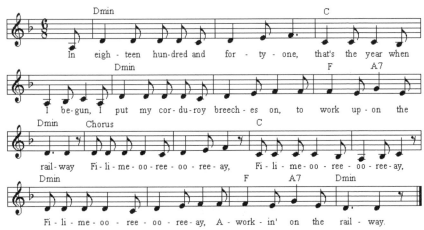

In eigh-teen hun-dred and for-ty-one, that's the year when I be-gun, I put my cor-du-roy breech-es on, to work up-on the rail-way. Fi-li-me-oo-ree-oo-ree-ay, Fi-li-me-oo-ree-oo-ree-ay, Fi-li-me-oo-ree-oo-ree-ay, A-work-in' on the rail-way.

Mt. Rainier Scenic Railroad

Photo by J.S. David Wilkie

The Respected Robber

One of the first train robberies in California was committed in 1870 by John T. Chapman, a respected member of the community and the superintendent of a Sunday school. The haul was $41,600 in gold coins. Chapman and his six companions were soon caught as they tried to spend their loot. All were sentenced to prison.

Paddy Works on the Railway

In eighteen hundred and forty-two,
I left the old world for the new;
I rue the luck that brought me through
While workin' on the railway.

In eighteen hundred and forty-three,
'Twas then I met sweet Biddy Magee;
An elegant wife she's been to me,
While workin' on the railway.

In eighteen hundred and forty-four,
Hands and feet were gettin' sore,
Hands and feet were gettin' sore,
From workin' on the railway.

In eighteen hundred and forty-five,
I found myself more dead than alive,
I found myself more dead than alive,
While workin' on the railway.

In eighteen hundred and forty-six,
I changed my trade to carryin' bricks,
I changed my trade to carryin' bricks,
From workin' on the railway.

In eighteen hundred and forty-seven,
Sweet Biddy Magee was sent to heaven,
If she left me a child, she left me eleven,
To work upon the railway.

"You're Hired!"

In 1853 Cornelius Vanderbilt was riding between Albany and New York on the Hudson River Railroad. He went to the baggage car to smoke a cigar, even though smoking was permitted only on the platform. The conductor, Allen Conrey, informed Vanderbilt of the rules, but Vanderbilt kept right on smoking. The conductor stuck to his guns and insisted that Vanderbilt refrain from smoking in the baggage car. Vanderbilt so liked Conrey's manner and persistence that he bought the entire railroad just to have Conrey work for him.

The Railroad Blues

I n case you are fantasizing about quitting your day job to become a hobo, here are the essentials of hobo lingo.

Riding the blinds: The "blind" was the space between the baggage car and the locomotive. Because baggage cars did not have a door on the forward end, they were "blind."

Riding the rods: Skinny hobos sometimes laid in the 18" space between the underside of a boxcar and the rods, which were part of the frame. This was a dangerous and noisy way to travel.

Riding the bumpers: The bumpers were the coupling joints between the cars. It was best to ride the bumpers after dark, when a brakeman might not notice you.

Riding the deck: In good weather, some hobos rode the deck, or the top of a baggage car. If a hobo fell asleep while riding the deck, he would likely roll off and be killed.

Riding the boxcars: The boxcar was the Motel 6 of hobo travel. Out of the wind, hobos often built fires on the boxcar floor, burning anything combustible, and sometimes the floor itself.

If you think hoboing was always a free ride, think again. If caught by a brakeman, you could be forced to fork over what little money you had. The going rate in the 1890's was about ten cents per one hundred miles, or twenty cents for an all night ride.

The Railroad Blues

Got the railroad blues, the railroad blues,
I got no heart to cry.
Got the railroad blues, the railroad blues,
I haven't got a dime.
I squandered all my money on the women and the booze.
The rest I spent it foolish 'til there's nothing left to lose,
Got the railroad blues, the railroad blues,
I got no railroad fare, I got no railroad fare.

Got the railroad blues, the railroad blues,
I'm ridin' down the railroad track.
Got the railroad blues, the railroad blues,
I ain't even lookin' back,
I'm leavin' all my worries and my troubles far behind
If the brakeman sees me hidin' I may have to ride the blinds,
Got the railroad blues, the railroad blues,
I got no railroad fare, I got no railroad fare.

Got the railroad blues, the railroad blues,
I'm flaggin' down the Santa Fe.
Got the railroad blues, the railroad blues,
I'll soon be on my way,
I can see your towns a-passing through the boxcar door
I'm leavin' this town won't be back no more,
Got the railroad blues, the railroad blues,
I got no railroad fare, I got no railroad fare.

R. Douglas Walker Collection

Durham & Southern Railway

Railroad Superstition

When a railroad man is killed, two more will follow before the charm is broken.

Train Trivia

It's Raining Money!

Oune Pullman porter was returning to his car with an armload of shoes he had just shined. He got the surprise of his life when he discovered that the aisle of his car was littered with one hundred dollar bills! It turned out that one of his passengers had hidden the money in his shoes, and then thoughtlessly left them out to be shined. The bills spilled out when the porter gathered the shoes to shine.[16]

Finders Keepers, Losers Weepers

In the gold-rush town of Deadwood, South Dakota, workmen were surprised to discover $1,200 in twenty-dollar bills when they dismantled an old railroad depot.[16]

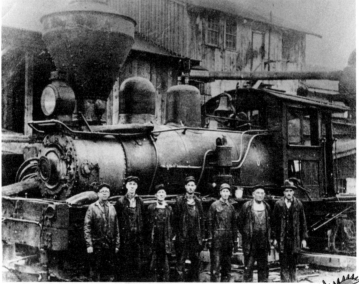

Jerry Ledford Collection

Moose Trouble

In Alaska, railroads often had moose trouble. The huge animals would get on the track and sometimes run for miles just ahead of the train. If the engineer sounded his whistle, the moose was likely to turn around and charge the engine.[16]

Oops!

The list of forgotten items left on trains begins with briefcases, wallets and golf clubs and ends with canary birds and homing pigeons.

Train Trivia

One passenger suddenly remembered that she had left her electric iron plugged in when she left the house. At the next station, the conductor called the police, who drove to the lady's home and unplugged the iron.

Yep

Telegraphers were so used to communicating in dots and dashes that they often were accused of speaking in monosyllables!

The Last Wood Burner

America's last commercial railroad to operate on wood was the Mississippi & Alabama Railroad. Its tender held just enough wood to run to the next refueling station, five miles down the line. The M & A continued to operate until the end of World War II.

"Pay Up Bub!"

An early New Hampshire law, later repealed, required railroads to pay farmers their asking price to cross their lands.

"You're Fired!"

James G. Hill, the railroad builder, once fired an office worker because he didn't like his name, "Spittles".

A Good Year For Bad Men

In 1895 there were no fewer than forty-three successful train robberies in the far West.

Not in the Rain!

In the early 1830's, when railroading was in its infancy, strange beliefs held sway. The magnificent locomotive *Old Ironsides* was considered inoperable in the rain, and was kept in its barn in inclement weather. A team of stout horses took its place!

Red and Green Signal Lights

"Papa - Did you wind your watch?" **Found on the tombstone of conductor Charles B. Gunn, Colorado Springs, Colorado**

Some people call them "tear jerkers," but I'd rather refer to the songs of heart-felt emotion from the turn of the century as "sentimental ballads." A good example of this kind of song is "Red and Green Signal Lights." The original title was "Just Set a Light," as copyrighted in 1896 with words by Henry V. Neal and music by Gussie L. Davis. Its first recording was in February, 1926, by Vernon Dalhart who recorded it for three different record companies. This version was taken from the G.B. Grayson and Henry Whitter's July 31st, 1928 recording for Victor. You can sing the lyrics at the top of page 59 as a chorus.

A little child on a sick bed lay, And to death seemed very near. Her parents' pride and the only child, Of a railroad engineer. His duty called him from those he loved, While the lights in his home burned dim, And while tears he shed, to his wife he said, "I will leave two lanterns trimmed."

THE WORLD'S BEST SALESMAN

Two salesmen aboard a Southern Pacific train were boasting as to who was the best salesman.

"You may not believe this," said the first salesman, "but on the day before I left, I sold $50,000 worth of boxes to General Electric."

"That's nothing," said the second salesman. "The day before I left, a woman came into my clothing store to buy a suit to bury her husband in, *and I sold her an extra pair of pants!*"[24]

Red and Green Signal Lights

Just set a light, when I pass tonight,
Set it where it can be seen,
If our darlin's dead, then show the red,
If she's better, show the green.

In a cottage home by the railroad side,
'Twas the mother's watchful eye,
Saw a gleam of hope in the feeble smile,
As the train went rushing by.
Just one short glance, 'twas his only chance,
But the signal light was seen,
On the midnight air, there arose a prayer,
"Thank God, the light is green."

How To Pour a Bottle Of Beer

Pullman porters underwent such strict training that two entire pages of the *Pullman Service Manual* were devoted to the proper procedure for serving a bottle of beer.

Sprout & Burn

Short on wood for fuel on the Nebraska prairie, railroad firemen were often forced to burn the only wood available, green cottonwood. Some engineers swore it actually sprouted even after it was fed into the firebox.

The Secret Code Of Porters

Porters have been known to signal each other when Pullman inspectors were nosing about. By holding the red cover of a magazine against a window, a porter could announce to a passing train that inspectors were making the rounds.

Believe it or Not!

A golf ball that landed in an open boxcar of a moving train traveled 300 miles and then came back to its owner. O.P. Seeman, an agent of the Canadian National Railway, was golfing when his ball disappeared after a tee shot. Several days later he received his ball back in the mail. A fellow agent found the ball in the car and mailed it back to him.[16]

WAKE UP!

A man was fast asleep in the corner of a street car. The conductor shook him and said, "What street do you want?" The man opened one eye and said, "What streets do you have?"

R. Douglas Walker Collection

Dear Sirs:

This letter was written to a railroad company by a sufferer who lived too close to a railway yard:

Gentlemen:

Why is it that your switch engine has to ding and gong and fizz and spit and bang and hiss and pant and grate and grind and puff and chug and bump and hoot and toot and whistle and wheeze and jar and jerk and howl and snarl and puff and growl and thump and boom and clash and jolt and screech and snort and snarl and slam and throb and roar and rattle and yell and smoke and smell and shriek like hell the whole night long?[22]

Stick 'Em Up!

Two friends were passengers on the Cactus Branch Railroad when their train was boarded by a masked man brandishing two six-shooters. "This is a hold-up!" he yelled. "Stick 'em up!" Before either of the friends could respond to the outlaw's demands, one of them reached in his pocket, pulled out a ten dollar bill, and handed it to his friend, saying, *"Here's the ten bucks I owe you."*[22]

Hog Wash

A Mississippi farmer sent this poem to the railroad:

My razor-back roamed your track
   A week ago today.
Your Number Nine came down the line
   And snuffed his life away.

You can't blame me; the hog, you see,
   Strolled through a cattle gate.
So kindly pen a check for ten,
   This debt to liquidate.

The claim agent's response:

Our Number Nine came down the line
   And killed your hog, we know.
But razor-backs on railroad tracks
   Quite often come to woe.

Therefore, my friend, we cannot send
   The check for which you pine.
Just bury the dead, plant o'er his head,
   "Here lies a foolish swine."[16]

The Devil's Road

While some early preachers feared the railroad was the devil's road, others claimed railroads actually made people *more* religious. After all, many a nervous passenger said their prayers when trains reached the unheard of speed of twenty-five miles an hour.

Keep Quiet!

"I went out for a street car ride. A drunk man got on the car. An old lady got up and said, "Conductor, do you allow drunken people to ride this car?" The conductor replied, "Yes, just sit down and keep quiet and no one will notice you."[23]

Railroad Superstition
It is an evil omen to step into the engine cab with your left foot first.

Working on the New Railroad

A folk song is like an empty boxcar rattling down the track. At every freight yard the cars are loaded and unloaded, and never stay the same for very long. So it is with "Working on the New Railroad."

Like a rolling boxcar, the song doesn't stay put but is always on the go, being passed from one singer to another, changing as it goes.

The earliest I have been able to trace the chorus of "Working on the New Railroad" is to the 1870's. The trail leads us to Fort Smith, Arkansas where a poor soul was awaiting execution from a hangman's noose. The hangman's name was George Maledon, and he personally hanged sixty unlucky men before he hung up his rope. He was carrying out the sentence handed down by the Honorable Isaac Charles Parker, known as the hanging judge."

As it is commonly sung, "Working on the New Railroad" is an odd collection of verses which combines the themes from "John Henry," advice for the lovelorn, and the final words of a condemned man. I have rearranged and composed new lyrics to the song.

Chorus

Hang me, oh ha-ng me and I'll be dead and gone, Hang me, oh ha-ng me and I'll be dead and gone, It ain't the hang-ing that I mind, it's lay-in' in the jail so long, I been all a-round this world.

Sleeping on the Job

One day, while walking down the track, the foreman of a gang of railroadmen discovered one of his men fast asleep under the shade of a tree. "Sleep on, my friend, sleep on. As long as you sleep, you've got a job, but when you awake, you're fired!"[21]

Working on the New Railroad

Working on the new railroad
With mud up to my knees, (2x)
Working for big John Henry,
And he's so hard to please,
I been all around this world.

Up on the Clinchfield Railroad,
It's there I'll take my stand (2x)
With a rifle on my shoulder,
Six-shooter in my hand,
I been all around this world.

The new railroad is ready, boys,
The cars are on the track, (2x)
They're takin' me down to Georgia,
But they ain't a-gonna bring me back,
I been all around this world.

The Staff of Ignorance

A switchman's job was to link and unlink the cars by using a hickory staff that was known as a "Brakeman's Club," or "The Staff of Ignorance." One trainman snuck up behind a gunman who refused to pay his fare and used his "Staff of Ignorance" as a "persuader." It turned out the outlaw had a price on his head, and the trainman collected a $2,000 reward.

R. Douglas Walker Collection

Flying Railroads!

"Railroads are positively the greatest blessing that the ages have wrought out for us. They give us wings; they annihilate the toil and dust of pilgrimage; they spiritualize travel!"
Nathaniel Hawthorne, *The House of Seven Gables.*

Railroad Superstition

If your hat blows off, it is a sign you will be sorry you started on your journey.

Thanks!

The hard-working train crew deserves credit for help in keeping me on track: Mack Kennikel, Bill Mill, Doug Walker, Norm Cohen, Barbara Swell, Janet Swell, Tracy McMahon, Justin Hallman, Pam Budd, Will Pruett, Steve Millard, O. Winston Link, Warren Wilson College Library, John & Lori Erbsen.

R. Douglas Walker Collection

Sources

1. *The Train That Never Came Back and Other Railroad Stories* by Freeman H Hubbard, 1952; 2. *Railroad* by James Alan McPherson and Miller Williams, 1976; 3. Collected by Vance Randolph; 4. *Slow Train Through Arkansas* by Thomas W. Jackson, 1904; 5. *The Locomotive Engineer*, April 4, 1975; 6. *5600 Jokes for all Occasions* by Mildred Meiers and Jack Knapp; 7. *The Age of Steam* by Lucius Beebe & Charles Clegg; 8. *Rail, The Records* by John Marshall, 1985; 9. *The Railroaders* by Stuart Leuthner, 1983. 10. *The Romance of the Rails* by Agnes C. Laut, 1929; 11. *On a Fast Train* by Thomas W. Jackson, 1905; 12. *Cowtown Columnist* by Boyce House, 1946; 13. *Glamorous Days*, Frank H Bushick, 1934; 14. *Language of the Railroader* by Ramon F. Adams, 1977; 16. *True Book of American Railroads* by Robert N. Webb, 1957; 17. *The Day They Hung the Elephant* by Charles Edwin Price, 1992; 18. *Pennsylvania Songs and Legends* by George Korson, 1949; 19. *Great Train Robberies of the West* by Eugene B. Black, 1959; 20. *Railroad Avenue* by Freeman H. Hubbard, 1945; 21. *A Treasury of Railroad Folklore* ed. B.A. Botkin and Alvin F. Harlow; 22. *Rail Life, A Book of Yarns* by Alfred Price, 1925; 23. *Through Missouri on a Mule* by Thomas W. Jackson, 1904; 24. *Laughing Stock* by Bennett Cerf, 1945.